SEMANTIC HYGIENE

SONGS OF MIRTH & MENACE

---

by
Ryan S. Leavitt

Semantic Hygiene

Ryan S. Leavitt

Cover art by Anna Kira, Sara Scioneaux
Illustrations by Dandi Pratama

If you enjoy your experiences in these pages, please consider leaving a review for this book on Amazon.

Visit my website at:
www.ryansleavitt.com

Also by Ryan S. Leavitt:

Writer, Seeker, Killer

THE FELLED
Never Going Back
Pure Intention
Protect Me From What I Want (Forthcoming)

As Ryan Starbloak:

GOD & everything
First Reality
This Never Happened Somewhere
Swiftopia
Funny Looks On a Serious Face
The Alternative Wrong

Contents

Introduction

1.

For my entire adult life, I've had a relationship with creativity. This relationship has had several distinct phases. At first, it was a curiosity; a distraction. Then to convert suffering into beauty. A survival mechanism. I wouldn't concede to the idea that art came from anywhere other than the things lacking in life. Thank goodness I snapped out of that. I think of it now as a compulsion. I'm sure this relationship and its dynamics will continue to unfurl into unanticipated paths, unspeakable tangents and dalliances.

My ten-year anniversary of publishing online was coming around, and I knew I wanted to commemorate it. I had already put out a collection of lyrics from my work as a musician. I didn't want to just do that over again. Something more called for. Brighter. More particular.

After several ideas, I abandoned the notion. Actually, I felt it was time to take a minor break from books altogether. The latest installment of *The Felled* had just come out. The scope of the project had me more drained than ever. I spent some time in real life, away from Arqa. There were a few things I'd always wanted to do, so I focused on that. For instance, there was a band I had always wanted to see play live, more than any other: From Autumn to Ashes.

Many factors have conspired against me over the years, which made seeing them unactionable. For one, they had disbanded by the time I knew of them. Eight years later, they were doing a reunion show in New York City. I made my way there from New Orleans, only to find out upon arrival that they had canceled the event. *Another* eight years went by. I saw they were playing in Boston, at the same venue where I had seen my first 18+ show. Determination rose in me—I *had* to go. The conspiracy seemed to persist. Would you believe my flight was redirected to Atlantic City because of a storm? With Logan Airport closed, the only option I had to arrive on time was a bus.

Obstacles surmounted, I made it, first venturing to the merch table for something that would always recapitulate what I knew was going to be one of the most anticipated moments of my life. I found something unexpected: a vinyl EP of frontman Francis Mark's solo material. Recorded a year before.

I should have known about this, I thought. *How could I* not *have known about this?* I regularly checked their profiles online —this released hadn't been announced. It was a very clandestine thing. I had always hoped for a solo effort from Francis. I would have had no idea about this new EP if I hadn't gone to Boston. I was sad that I didn't know it existed, but so hyped to discover it.

It was the first vinyl I ever bought. There was no other format available. I looked at the back of mine; written there was 56/200. There was no title, but the red cover had some streaks of black and white that Francis had applied with his painter's hands to each copy, along with his autograph at the center of the record.

I accepted the task of transporting this found object from Boston to New Orleans, knowing I would handle it like a baby at the airport, on the plane, the ride home. I didn't even have a vinyl player—fortunately, my roommate did. It would be about a week before I could listen to it. In the meantime, there was a sheet of lyrics included. It was just about the only time I *read* the lyrics to songs before to listening to them.

From Autumn to Ashes put on a memorable show. I will always be a little happier than I was before because of it.

I thought more and more about that vinyl. The implied anti-Spotify/streaming sentiment. The genuine appreciation of an artist and what we do to show it. Then everything clicked for me. *Something more*. How cool would it be to give someone else the experience of music, lyrics first? Extremely.

It couldn't be the exact same. I don't have the same notoriety as they do. Still, I feel there is a unifying factor: quality. I feel very confident that you can appreciate my songs solely from the lyrics, or by listening to the music that I have built around the words. I approach each composition as a lyricist first. Everything else emerges from that.

With that settled, I moved on to the next question... how could it be done?

That's what you're holding in your hands. *Semantic Hygiene* is an ongoing multimedia project that extends beyond these pages. If you buy the book, you will also have access to download the recorded songs. Presently, I have two musical projects: an alt-rock band, Allision, and a singer-songwriter outfit, The Every Year.

This is an opportunity for you to have the same "reversed" experience that I had with that vinyl. Only, I had five songs waiting for me. You will have dozens (beyond the dozen already uploaded) materializing. The private URL to the songs is in the back of the book. Every set of lyrics considered for inclusion here is ready to be recorded. The only prohibitive factor at the moment is recording expenses. And so buying this book is taking part in that intention. Supporting my books augments my ability to produce more, sooner.

If you think this proposition is nifty enough, then you know what to do.

2

I have already explained *what* this book is. Here comes the *why*. Lately, I've gained a lot of clarity about what I wish to accomplish with my art. Many artists detest explaining themselves, feeling threatened that self-commentary will diminish interest or narrow interpretation. I've settled this dilemma through compromise. The themes of my writing are things I want people to discern for themselves overall. Though there is one theme I wish to openly expose.

Most philosophies are abstract. Enjoyable puzzles of the mind that fascinate and enchant. But they do nothing to solve the problems of our species. Off the top of my head, I can think of only two pragmatic philosophies which, if genuinely adopted, could dramatically improve the functioning of our world. One is the mass adoption of sustainable housing (like Earthships). The other is general semantics.

Sadly, neither of these are immediately appealing prospects. There is little incentive to change our current system of housing (despite the non-inclusive, self-defeating nature of the whole thing). As for general semantics, it is very dry. Academic. *Horrendous* first date material. Still, I can trace many modern techniques relating to bettering one's mental health to the founder of general semantics, Alfred Korbyski.

Therapy is the attempt to train already dysfunctional people into having a better sense of feeling themselves. It is necessary, and more people should do it... but frankly, it's damage control. Not nearly as effective as if we could teach people from a very young age the concept of "the map is not the territory" to the point of understanding and application. I'm not saying I haven't benefited from therapy, only we would better serve issues by addressing causal sources earlier on.

Almost everybody can agree that the thing they sit on is not the five-letter word c-h-a-i-r. Not in sound or shape. It is only a constructed label for reference. Or that the description of the food they see on the menu is not what they will eat after ordering. These things are unanimous, yet still, people fail to recognize the larger implications of this point. We over-identify with our emotions and, by default, are possessed by the need for certainty. It's not possible to escape these linguistic constructs. However, general semantics is a method with which to better manage them. My work is my way of spreading this message above all else. To start people down the path of critical thinking. To become conscious that we never *understand* the world, we only *abstract* minuscule parts of it. And those parts are selected largely by choice. In the words of Tony Robbins, "Where focus goes, energy flows. And where energy flows, whatever you're focusing on grows."

Korzybski's answer is the training of non-allness. We must attempt to remember that far below this mapped world, there are only probabilities. The universe does not operate under the physics described by Aristotle, and yet our language is still based on Aristotelean principles. It is time to update our linguistic understanding to match the science of quantum mechanics. A good starting point more information on this is Robert Anton Wilson's *Quantum Psychology*.

3.

Now for a little housekeeping. The "..." symbol comes up often in these pages. It denotes an instrumental break, bridge, or solo. If it comes up twice, then the previously written chorus repeats. I did this a few times in the interest of saving trees, having two to four lines take up a whole new page seemed worse than occasionally abridging lyrics that repeat anyway. In "Suicidols", the "and" of the world is not a typo—but a pun. I think it's delightful how often someone says the world is going to end but then it doesn't. Seriously, there's a whole Wikipedia article on predicted apocalyptic events that never came to pass. One of them has got to be right eventually, but if they've all been wrong so far, why bother with the specificity?

I have also speckled some essays throughout this book which document some of the most seminal moments I've experienced as a songwriter. May they inspire you to be more creative in whatever it is you do or wish to do.

This book is somewhat experimental... I'm treading new territory as an artist in combining elements outside of the physical book. I want to thank you for participating in this fresh idea with me. We are in an age of reboots, reunion tours, and weaponized nostalgia... new ideas are dying. Most were never worth getting out there, but some are *very* beautiful. Amazon reviews are vital to my success (sad as that sounds), so if you enjoy what you read, please consider leaving a brief review of *Semantic Hygiene* there.

There will be an ongoing newsletter you can sign up to to stay updated on the progress of this project. There is also my Instagram, Theeveryyear, and my YouTube channel, Ryan S. Leavitt.

I play with words, knowing they are only perceptions. I play with words for the joy of laughter and connection. I play with words, but I do not believe they are the things they represent. I play with words to remind myself of all this. My hope is that the aftermath of this play has a similar effect on you.

WARNING:
High Concentrations
of Mirth & Menace

Acknowledgments

To my direct collaborators: Love Danielson, Eric Carter, Robert Johannessen, MK, Jordan Cooperman, Missing Teeth, Keith Johnson... it has been unspeakably incredible working and growing with y'all! I want to give attributions here: Love Danielson co-wrote parts of "Mountain Don't", "Walpurgisnacht", "Break Glass Lover", and "Terminally Gullible". Eric Carter wrote the music on "Optimism", "Oddessey", and "Suncheck" and the titles, while I wrote the lyrics. Same is true for Jordan Cooperman, who wrote "Stuck", and Keith Johnson on "Back In the Day" & "Utterly Resistible".

Let me also make mention of some of the many influences that have moved me to write some of the pieces in this collection or have helped to shape my approach to writing: Timothy Leary, Lindsey Buckingham, Robert Anton Wilson, David Lynch, Hajime Isayama, Antero Alli, Tony Robbins, Nobuo Uematsu, Robert Pirsig, Mark Frost, Daron Malakian, Hideaki Anno, T. Duggins, Raphael Bob-Waksberg, Alfred Korzybski, Kentaro Muira, Max Collins, Brian Fuller, Rob Potylo, Dorothy Parker, Janeane Garofalo, Michael Reynolds, Rebecca Sugar, Shirley Manson, Regina Spektor, Yoshihiro Togashi, Voltaire, Carl Jung, Billy Corgan, Patrick Rothfuss, Jhonen Vazquez, Joss Whedon, Francis Mark, Meg Frampton, Dia Frampton, Woody Allen, Brian Molko, Gen Urobuchi, Kentaro Muira, Tetsuya Nomura.

& let's not forget Jordan Peterson for his tireless work in the field of seeming like such a twat (to me).

MYSTERIOUS & REASSURING

I'm so blissed off, commence the gambling
May not return here for a spell
Took lengthy ganders at those peepers
The feeling's flung, so unfair-well

One with the rushing of the water
Body is rotting in a dell
Ah shit, but I just bought those sneakers
Under the sun, my trinkets melt

Mysterious & reassuring
Fearless, my one character flaw
It's not the falling or the landing
Jumping's what I like most of all

If you're thinking I deserve the credit
Then I'd say expect to have a fit
Riddled, so void of past resplendence
Due to external incidents

Mysterious & reassuring
Fearless, my one character flaw
It's not the falling or the landing
Jumping's what I like most of all

...

Mysterious & reassuring
Fearless, my one character flaw
It's not the falling or the landing
Jumping's what I like most of all

Mysterious & reassuring
Fearless, my one character flaw
It's not the finding or the keeping
Yearning's what I like most of all
('Cause yearning's irresponsible)

ENGAGED

We got engaged, got engaged in shenanigans
Wed, no I jest, maladjusted of course I am
They built a cage, built a cage, so we're not having kids
Common and sense separated, where have they went?

I used to feel hate
For all the red states
But that's no way to be
Delusionality

The freest speech benefits more intolerance
Drives, yes, it drives, it drives sales when the books are banned
Think it'd be nifty if we held hands on this ledge
Give me a selfie, your soul, & your brain damage

I used to feel hate
For all the red states
But that's no way to be
Delusionality

I live, I live off the fat of the land
But this land's obese and diseased, needs some medicine

...

I used to feel hate
For all the red states
But that's no way to be
Der Gazpacho police

THE SUN EXPLODING

When the sun blows
It'll take eight minutes to know
When your looks fades
The damage cannot be reversed

They are flowing, the juices of war
Yet the spit in your mouth isn't yours
Took billions and billions of years
But now we are finally not here

When your face melts
May you not learn what's in store
We're all set here
Till our atoms are flicked and disturbed

They are flowing, the juices of war
Yet the suds in your mouth aren't yours
Took billions and billions of years
At last we are finally not here

Societal Pressure Disorder

To tell you the truth I'm not
Who taught you how to smile?
For each little thing
Abandoned house but clean tile

Judging from the grass
Wholesale sold your bile
Soiled, sunken flag
Our history clues your guile

Petrol almost gone
Traded in for air
Snap the final twig
Fumes we must inhale

Aimed right for the mouth
We were so unruly
So awfully unruly, truly
Had to hoist us out
Broken fists so drooly
Bloody no duh, absolutely

Your gravity's so distinct
You lavender-scented fire
Puppet posed to wink
Success has failed your child

Damned for what you damn
Pageantry defined
Contact trace your skin
Your choice not to decide

Aimed right for the mouth
We were so unruly
So awfully unruly, truly
Had to hoist us out
Broken fists so drooly
Bloody no duh, absolutely

...

Punching our own mouths
We were so unruly
So awfully unruly, truly
Had to hoist us out
Broken fists so drooly
Bloody no duh, absolutely

Scoobie, scoobie, doobie
Scoobie, scoobie, scoobie, doobie
Scoobie, scoobie, doobie... do

STAY GORGEOUS, GET DREAMY

Touch isn't what you think
It's electrons repelling
Endured like a critique
Force field from the shelling

I was lifted where you knelt
Supremely alluring
Snappy with the, "Do tell."
You can't fake being boring

There's a chasm in my mind
There's a goal I'll never reach
I'm made of star stuff, once so bright
How is your mystery?

Rearview's all that you see
Force words while you're yawning
Stay gorgeous, get dreamy
You can't need what you're wanting

Rearview's all that you see
Stay gorgeous, get dreamy

There's a chasm in my mind
There's a goal I'll never reach
I'm made of star stuff, once so bright
How is your mystery?

Facts now soon may be untrue
Certainty's beyond belief
Look it up, spacetime is doomed
No, I still don't wanna meet

...

There's a chasm in my mind
There's a goal I'll never reach
I'm made of star stuff once so bright
How is your mystery?

Fallen wyverns that we'd ride
There's a girl I'll never meet
Composed of supernova shards
But I lack the memory

(Lessons Learned in Lynn, Part 1)

As a teenager, I covered my desk in clips and lines from my favorite songs. I once printed out every song I could find from the band Otep and hung them in my room. I would go on azlyrics.com to find non-album tracks of my favorite bands. Sometimes with those rare songs, the lyrics were all you could find. It made you wonder if the songs existed at all or if agents of Eris posted them.

The opposite would happen on Myspace. All these ephemeral bands posting exceptional music recorded in a bathroom, with the lyrics nowhere to be found. One salient example of this was "Betwixt Her Getaway Sticks" by From Autumn to Ashes. I had to message them to find out what the words were. They messaged back with about 90% of the words, but they couldn't remember a few lines. I love that notion. That possibility that I valued the lyrics to this song more than the person who wrote it.

Free Determinism

I've been free
Unhealthy
No more schemes
I'm just kidding

All that you motivate
Always a Saturday
The things you label hate
You're just reading

If I say water
While you die of thirst
If I say power
I'm still unheard

The map we made up
Is not the world
Seems like you'd kill for
Metaphor

'Is' of identity
Helps me bleed
Tricks I think
The word is not the thing

Abstractions made a
Robotic serf
Substantive knowledge
Soil the Earth

This stuff you've made up
Is, "Oh your god..."
Imagine Dragons
To your pity fuck

...

Abstractions made one
Immune to health
Let's flip the script &
Toil the wealth

This stuff you've made up
Is, "Oh your god..."
Imagine Dragons
To your pity fuck

WEAPONIZED NOSTALGIA 3: OUR SEQUEL

Pursuant lilting and reeking of fiction
I lie, oh, to prevent his harm
Boisterous tilting with corporal risking
So calm... and pleasant when wrong

Recent addictions make memories go missing
I trace those you once regaled
Cherish this ceiling on documents fearing
The leverage you folded to sail

I'm willingly unable
You're gratefully unstable
Cursed to afford this cable
Receive your texts like rainbows

Is it still true that you laugh
When you're lying, lying, lying?
Is it just a rumor you carried it off?

Cautious endearment of optional suspects
Assume guilt to be who you blame
Target fulfillment, then settling for just
A chance to love you too late

I wanna show you painful
Your peacefulness is evil
No halves are ever equal
Don't wanna make our sequel

Is it still true that you laugh
When you're lying, lying, lying?
Is it just a rumor you carried it off?

Underneath the willow that's drying
That's drying, drying, drying
Lose control of the flame meant for the moths

...

Is it still true that you laugh
When you're lying, lying, lying?
Is it just a rumor you carried it off?

Underneath the willow that's drying
That's drying, drying, drying
Lose control of the flame meant for the moths

Yes, in fact you need drugs for crying
For crying, crying, crying
No, I don't know what "subjective" it means

Hurtling reboots and new ideas
Dying, dying, dying
Weaponized nostalgia that cracks both my knees
(Weaponized nostalgia won't address your needs)

Any Questions?

I got my elementary school
Report cards in a box
Never realized how transparent
My maladjustment was

I had a violent streak
Coerce me to suppress my rage
But now I censor most of all
Of what I need to say

I wasn't popular but
I did have a little niche
But that belonging went away
And it is torturous

Since we went opposite ways
The color of the flame
I won't, I won't waver
Your answer is a shame
We'll have to keep away
I won't, I won't waver

Matter makes elements
Dysfunctional, composed of this
Friendships are formed
Under conditions of impermanence

Thoughtless inventions if
Connections never catalyze
Trusting the man much less
Than his animal's tragic eyes

Since we went opposite ways
Your pockets full of flames
I won't, I won't waver
Your answer is a shame
We'll have to keep away
I won't, I won't waver

...

Since we went opposite ways
The color of the flame
I won't, I won't waver
Your answer is a shame
We'll have to keep away
I won't, I won't waver

If You're Here,
Then Where Am I?

If you're here, then where am I?
The menu is the meal this time

She folds her day up like a sheet
Finding her happiness eerie

If you're here, then where am I?
Sub-atomic, double-blind

There is no up or down in space
Once I'm in danger, you'll be safe

Big things are coming
The sky's recorded
Big things are coming
Whole sky's recorded
(Can't unrecord it)

If you're me, then who am I?
Left is five & right are nine

She throws her night up in the sink
Just one more mishap voids the lease

If I live, then how'd I die?
Translinguistic, omnicide

...

Big things are coming
(Big things are coming)
The sky's recorded
(The sky's recorded)
Big things are coming
(Big things are coming)
Whole sky's recorded
(Whole sky's recorded)

Big things are coming
Sky's recording
Gee... oh

Havoc

It takes no time to theorize
Who you're targeting tonight
Inconvenience her and I
Pack the sword, the ax, the knives

What...
What'll it take for us to learn?
We bring havoc to it all
Havoc, steer to fall

Circle back to see how
Brash spirits impersonal
Explaining it to me now
Solitude so paramount

What...
What'll it take for us to learn?
We bring havoc to it all
Havoc, steer to fall

What...
What'll it take for us to learn?
We bring havoc to it all
Havoc, shift the fault

...

What...
What'll it take for us to learn?
We bring havoc to it all
Havoc, steer to fall

What...
What'll it take for us to learn?
We bring havoc to it all
Havoc, shift the fault
Havoc, suit no cause

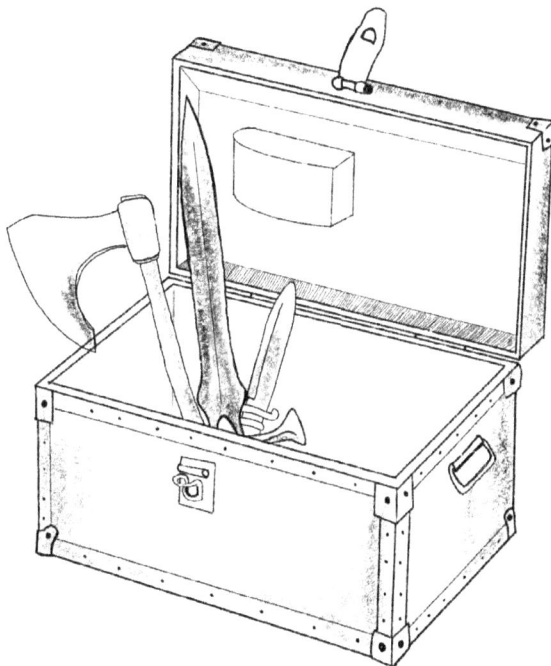

(Lessons Learned in Lynn, Part 2)

When I was first learning how to play the guitar, there was an urgency. A neediness that I thought would only be settled if I was "good." I made a list of the five songs I wanted to learn most: "The Fiction We Live" by From Autumn to Ashes, "Ana's Song" by Silverchair, "Early Sunsets on Monroeville" by My Chemical Romance, "Stay" by U2 (specifically Flyleaf's version), and "Santa Barbara" by Meg & Dia.

I managed to learn them all. At one point I posted a tab of the Meg & Dia song, since there wasn't an accurate one. I had to rely on my ears, training I received from a piano teacher in high school. These songs were my focus for a long time. If I could learn them, dissect them, and then create something original that was half as powerful, I might be sated.

I'm not sure if satiation has ever taken place for me, but I am having so much fun in the progression.

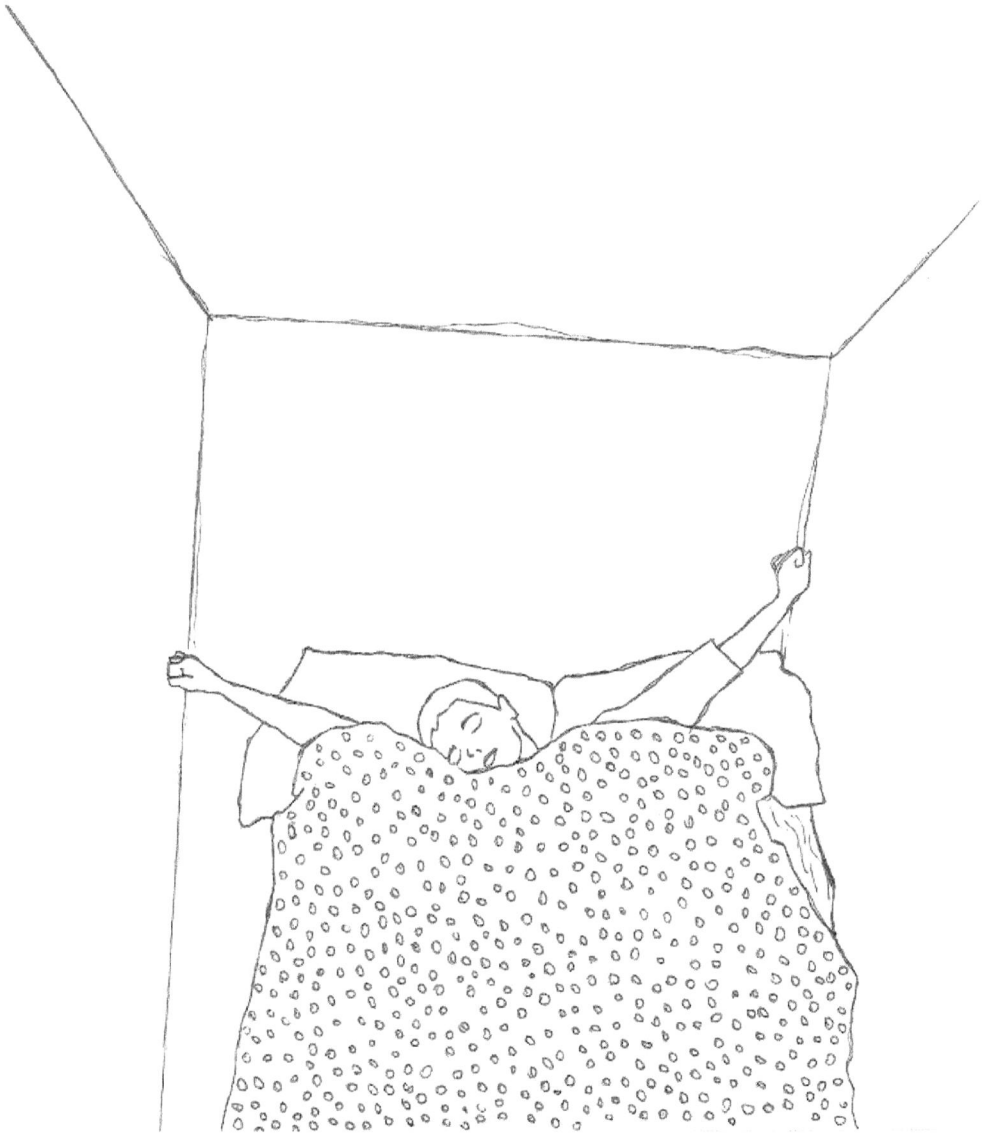

TRUE NORTH

Took years
To say
These words
Wrong brain
To gain
Heart's been
Clawing
It's way

They say that true north is a calling of sorts
We race to get out from the rain
But it is the worst, 'cause when it is known
It's what we've avoided to aim

And what we don't know, well, that is mutual
Become what I never became
The quietest gap revealing that lack
No love shall be tempered with shame

I found victory in exhaustion
Trees lost out on an unkept promise
Decision making; caveman level
Should evolve, but I know better

Said nothing matters meant the world to me
Respond, I take off my reality
And we discussed a union in space
We crashed the ship before we were made

They say that true north is a calling of sorts
We race to get out from the rain
But it is the worst, 'cause when it is known
It's what we've avoided to aim

And what we don't know, well, that is mutual
Become what I never became
The quietest gap revealing that lack
No love shall be tempered with shame
(Come on, are you not entertained?)

...

They say that true north is a calling of sorts
We race to get out from the rain
But it is the worst, 'cause when it is known
It's what we've avoided to aim

And what we don't know, well, that is mutual
Become what I never became
The quietest gap revealing that lack
No love shall be tempered with shame
(Come on, are you not entertained?)

Suicidols (The And of the World)

Retail stores closing, so don't change their minds
Paddle with me where the floods are tonight
Inattentive, her greenest of eyes
Gave it your best, but your best was just fine

Wants create shadows that freeze you inside
Hungry and horny for H bombs to shine
Uninventive, the calendar lines
The borders of boredom first blur, then they blind

Manufacturing
A fiction real as me

Suicidal
Little while
Candy aisle
I'm beside ya

They grift us the same way I fake throw a ball
To a dog darting we're all gullible
Glisten mellifluous, pasting your source
Abiogenesis, the and of the world

Suicidols
Tabloid trials
Candy aisle
Pinned beside ya now

Jordan Peterson Seems
Like Such a Twat To Me

One of the cruelest Canadians
Is a smart cookie
He could debate any college kid
But he can't tweet his beliefs

Gotta wonder why
Gotta wonder why
Critical thinking's gone

Gotta wonder why
Gotta wonder why
Critical fail

I'm generally much more well spoken with what I say
Jordan Peterson seems like such a twat to me
I loath resorting to calling someone a name, but
Jordan Peterson seems like such a twat to me

To me
To me
To me
To me

To me
To me
To me!

THAT LOUD

The sidewalk where she crashes with
Twisted fingers that never bent back again
Small town, Midwestern ashes
I didn't know she wasn't on the mend

On that Tuesday we sat down
Two years later, she gave out
The ink you'd saved for the pen you crowned
I'm not willing to get that loud

Wraith orbits 'round your spirit and
Siphons out precious oxygen
Untold machines are piloting
Feeling good to finally be stuck again

That Fat Tuesday we sat down
Two years later, truth came out
The ink you'd saved for the pen you crowned
I'm not willing to get that loud

Prototype fails to astound
Domestic aid that you withheld
The love you have for it drowns
I'm not willing to get that loud

...

On that Tuesday we sat down
Two years later, truth came out
The ink you'd saved for the pen you crowned
I'm not willing to get that loud

Prototype fails to astound
Domestic aid that you withheld
The love you have for it drowns
I'm not willing to get that loud

You smoke my disaster's risen cloud
I'm not willing to get that loud
The love you have for it drowns
I'm not willing to get that loud
(No, I'm not willing to get that loud)

Utterly Resistible

This poison
Tastes funny to me
Won't sway you to leave...

This poison, you see
Tastes funny to me
Won't sway you to leave
Won't sway you!

There's a lot, a lot I can't afford oh—
I've been stealing from a counterfeiter
Secret shakes and knocks, a speaker unknown
On the loose, undead I'm battlin'!

I don't wanna be a prisoner of happiness so
Don't be gentle; you should spill me over
I don't want to be enslaved to my experiences
When my ego's high, sweep my composure

In waiting, all these week long nights
A viscous, melting sky
Hell yes or no?!

Well, since you had asked to know me more uh—
Most times I'm utterly resistible, I—
Rig the light to make the shadow unfold
Sew me up once I'm unravelin'!

I don't wanna be a prisoner of happiness so
Don't be gentle; you should spill me over
Rather not be so ensnared by this much dopamine oh
Like the plummet from a high to sober

...

I don't wanna be a prisoner of happiness so
Don't be gentle; you should spill me over
I don't want to be enslaved to my experiences
When my ego's high, sweep my composure

Don't want you to be my primary antagonist, so
Please overcorrect, be mediocre
I don't want to be enslaved to my experiences
Just a time or two please claim it's over?

(Lessons Learned in Allston)

There's a video of me on the Internet being held down and spit on. No, it's not porn. Outsider artist Rob Potylo is bearing down on me, having a meltdown. Having one of the most important moments of your life recorded is really convenient.

Rob had invited me to guest star in an episode of his mockumentary, *Quiet Desperation*. After asking my mother if it was okay to skip school, I was good to go. I had been following Rob's career for years as he released album after album, video after video. Now I was going to be a part of it. We first connected directly through a whiny email I sent about getting dumped. Seeing as he had written a song called, "Hope I Get Something Creative Outta This", I imagined he'd know what to do. I still have his response hanging up in my room.

The story in the episode is I go to Rob's apartment to interview him for my high school newspaper. The interview triggers Rob into mania, then becomes a parody of that scene in *Fight Club* where Tyler Durden places lye on the protagonist's hand.

Instead of lye, it's Pop Rocks. Instead of accepting the knowledge of death, Rob's imperative is for me to admit that the universe doesn't care about what I create.

Yes, in the context of the show, it was all a joke. Rob was dialing up his character nearly to the brink of transforming into his brash alter ego, Robby Roadsteamer. But that moment shaped me. All that tumult and severity, that frustration from Rob, that came from a real place. A place I longed to be, no matter what became of me. I admired this person for being an artist uninhibited. Making what came from his mind with full conviction. Before that day, art was only a hobby to me. That scene was my initiation into the life I've lived ever since. A ritual confirming my devotion.

In the scene, I'm crying out through the pain, "I don't want to be an artist!"

Sometimes that's true. But I revere the scar that Pop Rocks pulp left on my hand.

Plotted Against

It once was believed
That there was no time
Before the Big Bang
Before clocks, before past

History's laden with
Unexplained vanishings
One of these days
I'll never come back

Your style of being
I find rather menacing
Nervous system signals
You may attack

I am convinced, yeah, they mean to do harm to me
My power's charging for it
There is this feeling, but was planted by them?
Why must it seem like I'm plotted against?

I am convinced, yeah, they mean to do harm to me
My power's charging for it
There is this feeling, but was planted by them?
Why must it seem like I'm plotted against?

The fossil record
Represents a minority
Most species die
With no trace and no tracks

Nothing and being are
Caught in a cavalcade
Something always
Pushing, shoving back

No city or creedo
Will outlast the entropy
No consciousness, common sense
Comic book death

I am convinced yeah, they mean to do harm to me
My power's charging for it
There is this feeling, but was planted by them?
Why must it seem like I'm plotted against?

I am convinced yeah, they mean to do harm to me
Like soon I'll no longer exist
There is this feeling, but was planted by them?
Why must it seem like I'm plotted against?

SUNCHECK

Wishing for your praise
In a real pathetic way
& I think back
To the time I traced

Your number on my arm
Both accomplished & alarmed
T minus way too soon
Till en garde

Dump me right off AIM
For the second time today
After I had walked
You home, it makes

Me wish we could talk
Maybe in person; log off
At the very least
You're off of my top 8

Screamed to fake sick from school
Gotta research paper due
& I don't feel like writing
Or reciting any *Iliad*

Forge sick notes in homeroom
Risky but I'll pull through
The cause is so exciting
It's inciting lots of silliness

Fires on the cliff
In the open, then we split
But the cops would
Find us in a jiff

Orange shirt I wore
Friends in camo, goth, concerned
All my crimes since
Prove that I haven't learned

The older that you age
Well the greater the mistake
Guess I'll have to
Run away in chains

Writing you a note
In a bottle & I hope
You remember me
Ah shit, oh wait, nope

Screamed to fake sick from school
Gotta research paper due
& I don't feel like writing
Or reciting any *Iliad*

Forge sick notes in homeroom
Risky but I'll pull through
The cause is so exciting
It's inciting lots of silliness

Black Hole

Tell me how your sister's been
Treated like a cigarette
Wavering my penance
Relishing in punishment

Differing her medicine
Fortified her garrison
Said her problem's anything
Punk rock, even sex is weak

No one looks cool
In the maw of black hole
Didn't want you to think
This isn't normal

Specimen so restless and
Dissect under heat lamp
Firing pain management
On your case while underfed

No one looks cool
In the maw of black hole
Didn't want you to think
This isn't normal

Invocations
You're so unforgivable
Looking right in your eyes
Is a chemical burn

DECONSTRUCTION

A clearing, your letters sail
We're not evacuating here
Once spanning, inversion near
You wager all that I can spare

This nausea, no turns without
A tower breaching through the clouds
Devotion, conviction, then doubt
The offer stands if you're allowed

That one'll often self-inflict
Her heart attacks my brain
World given to an astral slip
The noumenal is just a wave

One word that does not exist
Influenced violent zealousness
Evil with ideas unsaid
Heretical with every stance

Now standing in the way of death
Threats so insured by stony lips

That one'll often self-inflict
Her heart attacks my brain
World given to an astral slip
The noumenal is just a wave

No Judgement Day

If'n I was willing
To tell for a living
My way

That a consciousness
That's inherited
Is just vomiting

When the corporate art
Meets some of your needs
Petty

& folks who adore you
Swarm your house to
Lift your truth away

My Massachusetts burn
Radon in shallow dirt
Go with them or you will be afraid

Your dog was clutching a
Dead rabbit or possum
You can't control an animal enraged

If'n indecision ain't
A part of free will
But fate

Then the sun in the sky
Shall collect in my eyes
Outgrow my mistakes

I just wanna be
Myself for a living
My way

& waiting so long
For you to prove me wrong
It's no Judgement Day

My Massachusetts burn
Radon in shallow dirt
Go with them or you will be afraid

Your dog was clutching a
Dead rabbit or possum
You can't control an animal enraged

...

My Massachusetts burn
Radon in shallow dirt
Go with them or you will be afraid

Your dog was clutching a
Dead rabbit or possum
You can't control an animal enraged

Eldest Ghost

I chase it in dreams
The trembling sheets
Avoiding for keeps
And battling sleep

Enough hate for three
The fraction repeats
The last chance, agreed?
A cavalier meet

I'm still running away here at 8
Onto uncharted, passionate days
I've divested you, out of my way
I am the eldest ghost that you made

Wouldn't I notice your mispronounced consonants?
Why is every missive so lean?
I have been debating volitional consciousness
Choosing not to know what it means

Why is every action demanding of consequence?
What of retrocausality?
Shrinking repression from our shifting continents
There is finally healing to be

I'm still running away here at 8
I don't care if I ruin my legs
I've divested you, out of my way
I am the eldest ghost that you made

(Lessons Learned in Lynn, Part 3)

I caught this movie the other day, a group of writers around a dinner table talking about the trajectory of AI in human sexuality. Programming it to say whatever you need to get off. I think we all have a few things in mind. Shortcuts to elicit that sought-after orgasm.

There are things about ourselves we'd all like to hear, in bed or out of it. Certain compliments or things we want people to ask about us. The thing is, they can't just come from anybody.

Some people never get asked what they want, even from people who they wouldn't like to hear it from. Some people do, but since they were fishing for it, don't feel the full effect.

Once, I was told something about my music that I haven't been told since. By someone I admired. Best of all, it was something I didn't know I had wanted to hear, but once I did, I was illuminated. Of course, I'd like to hear it again, but I will never say what it was. It was one of the nicest things anyone's ever said to me.

WIL

Each atom of her body
That pill you want to be
Change isn't terrifying
When it happens gradually

Each sentimental offer
A quality defeat
You could slay a fucking monster
But you'll never achieve peace

Pleaded my significance
And figured out how to forget
If this is failing, let's not
Act as if we're sorry

Wish that I was in such debt
It's certainly no main event
Names of all who you have
Coerced into your evil

I'm finding in my vengeance
I'm losing in my sleep
My addiction made me happy
I was eternally

Pleaded my significance
And figured out how to forget
If this is failing, let's not
Act as if we're sorry

Wish that I was in such debt
It's certainly no main event
Names of all who you have
Coerced into your evil
Coerced into your evil
Wish that I weren't so
Coerced into your evil

ASUKA STRIKES!

You were the last worst decision I made
I'm sure of that
Faced me with all of your willingness, then
Unzipped your plaid

Two weeks we swooned, it make me think
But I was had
Love always will mingle with grief
To prove it lasts

The anima attacked me
Intestines do unfold
Ruthless and rarely sorry
Persona chemical

You were the best worst decision I made
On air we clashed
Emotional grenades, you hawked
Your aftermath

It was absurd to challenge
Your kind of wrath
Voices, you heard your name from the
Crowd in the back

The anima attacked me
Intestines, learn to crawl
Ruthless and rarely sorry
Project to your vessel

The danger's what attracts me
I'd risk another glance
If I could have your grace, please
Your paws can snap my neck

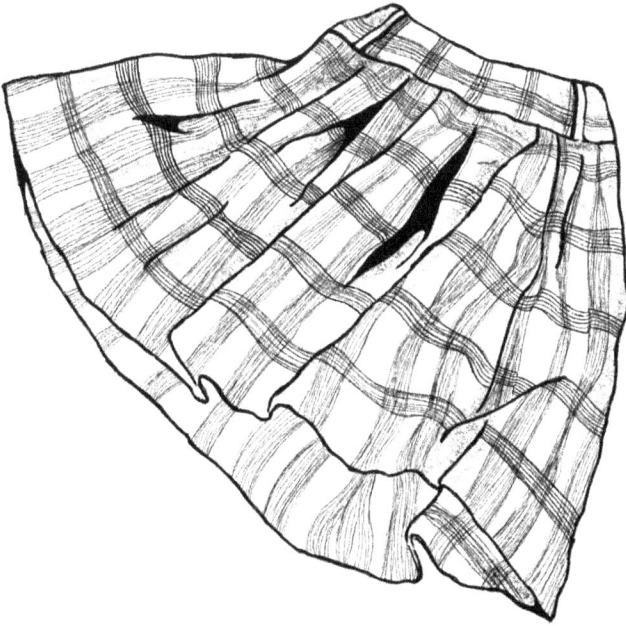

Seven Words

This isn't what I want you to mean to me
Ephemeral, in need
Somebody else that covertly operates
A cuteness unseen

For all that, she lacked your fire
And although it wasn't night
Transformed while she disarmed me
What man put up a fight?

Our fracas topples over their scenery
Don't listen or heed
A realm beyond foreshadows my final day
I got till next week

For all that, she lacked your fire
And although it wasn't night
Transformed while she disarmed me
What man put up a fight?

Just seven words required
No book will tell you how
She'll send her horde of demons
The fairest one for now

...

For all that, she lacked your fire
And although it wasn't night
Transformed while she disarmed me
What man put up a fight?

Just seven words required
No book will tell you how
There's repercussions, legions
The fairest one for now

MY PEARLNESS

My Pearlness has me
Way too close to codependency
I sing the perfect note
For Pink Diamond's elegy

She drank too much like
A Sugalite that's rampaging and
I sacrifice my peace of mind
All over Beach City

I am not fearless
Didn't mean to prove you wrong
I was at your service
But I'm moving on

I'm so imperfect but
I'll have you all know
I'm here, fucked up and all
To give you love to show

My Pearlness has me
Way too close to codependency
We waged a war and won
So I thought we'd get freaky

But she went on to choose a Greg
Because he's so burly and
I sacrifice my peace of mind
All over Beach City

I am not fearless
Didn't mean to prove you wrong
I was at your service
But I'm moving on

I'm so imperfect but
I'll have you all know
I'm here, fucked up and all
To give you love to show

Things Are Even More Normal
Now Than They Ever Were Before

Things are more normal now
Than they ever were before
Did you sense something weird
Was happening? No

Look within, lolz, j/k
Fall into a screen away
We can joke about doom
Maybe death is funny

Climate change my hair to grey
My blues red oxidized, bloody
Subsidiaries profiting
Virtual lets virtue waste

That is such a great question
You know I must not care
Polarized, what of friends?
Isolation to spare

Suffer it, abbreviate
We've got progress to escape
We should fuck without names
Maybe exchange money

Climate change my hair to grey
My blues red oxidized, bloody
Subsidiaries profiting
This is a human sprint, not race

Fly-go [sic]

Made it to the parking lot
Saw some guy there with a truck
Failed to sell a store his crates
Asked if he could demonstrate

The invention that he'd made
Don't call it that
Went high up as the billboard ad
Not a pogo stick, I was a kid
Couldn't buy it
Unsafe, I shoulda tried it

Said, "It's a Fly-go, kid."
Bounced upon the tarmac skid
Challenging Earth's gravity
Left me there so differently

The invention that he'd made
I told my mom
The dreamer and the product of
For a second there, held up midair
Couldn't get one
Just quarter bags of Funyons

... ...

THE CLOSEST FURTHER AWAY

We're surrounded by "eventuallies"
All this motion, microcosmic stains
Who inspires our activities?
Opposites clash, but they bitch the same

I wish you were further from me
The latest array
I'd prefer you further from me
Go light-years all day

His goodness kept his worst below
His greatness surfaces never
So few can ever have both
Evil persists and it lurks
Goodness, greatness
They seldom work—

Insight, it won't change who you'll be
Garbage alley, hobby is to wait
Don't outgrow that which is obsolete
Virtue legend, crises to invade

I wish you were further from me
I'd get it engraved
I'd prefer you further from me
The closest further away

His goodness kept his worst below
His greatness surfaces never
So few can ever have both
Evil persists and it lurks
Goodness, greatness
They seldom work

Together
Together
Together
Together

His goodness kept his worst below
His goodness surfaces never
So few can ever have both
Evil so hot that it flirts
Goodness, greatness
They seldom work

Together
Together
Together
Together

Janeane Garofalo

Your worst turn of phrase
Is better than any of their goddamn punchlines
No more 'seize the day'
Obnoxiously witty, acerbic, you're full time

Janeane, Janeane
I laugh at your wise ass, laugh at... you're wise
Janeane, Janeane
I laugh at your wise ass, laugh at... you're wise

She shudders with grace
In retrospect now, you've tousled and devised
Don't mind, lean away
Obnoxiously witty, acerbic, you're full time

Janeane, Janeane
I laugh at your wise ass, laugh at... you're wise
Janeane, Janeane
I laugh at your wise ass and savor your contrast

Jeaneane

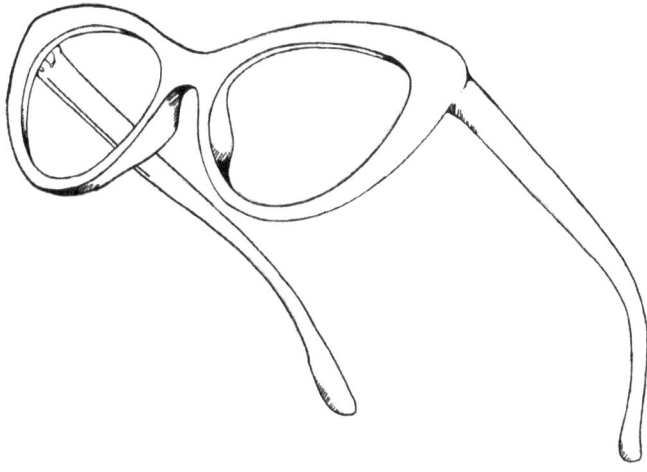

(Lessons Learned in Salem)

Early on in my first gig, the booker cut me off.

"This is a family establishment," he explained with a sour face. "You're gonna have to tone it down if you want to keep playing."

I reluctantly course-corrected... floundered is probably a better word. My material suddenly became unperformable. And I knew nothing else. What I always found strange was that I met this booker at an open mic, after having played a song about the moment in every person's life that comes shortly after discovering what sex is. That agonizing thought that your own parents, by deduction, must have done it for you to exist. The song had a sad, minor progression. But the lyrics were inane. Still, he'd booked me on that basis.

That was where I got my start in songwriting. Blue comedy. Late oos cringe humor. I did have the desire to be a comedian. But back then, it was more that I didn't want to be vulnerable. It was easier to get people's grossed-out reactions, laugh a bit, if I was lucky.

When I began to open up and write serious songs, they were worse than anything I had done before. But eventually, they got better. Much better.

If My Back Goes Out, I've Got My Mouth

You poured the flood in my hands
If squirt was piss, I'd understand
I don't want any of you
If it's to melt by summer
Belief, denial, source nor proof
Built from shattered terror

I'll play God if you play dumb
Never wearing pants alone
I'll play God if you play dumb
Curry favor, stadium

They ate the palm of your hand
Your fingers point nowhere again
Seen evading how you look
Credulity in tatters
Belief, denial, source nor proof
Built from shattered terror

I'll play God if you play dumb
(If my back goes out, I've got my mouth)
Never wearing pants alone
(If my back goes out, I've got my mouth)
I'll play God if you play dumb
(If my back goes out, I've got my—)
Curry favor, stadium

Blue Water Navy

They misread your paper freely
With a stone shoved down your throat
For what little you could mumble
Decide not to let them know

You're sleek and defenselessness baby
Your kindness was unstoppable
Phone in your blue water navy
The vote to authorize a go

Dude, I better not be preachy
Intelligence emotional
If the analytics baffle
Impose upon another host

You're sleek and defenseless, baby
Your kindness was unstoppable
Phone in your blue water navy
The vote to authorize a go

...

I'm a diplomat, I'm crazy
The attack on me is on
Go down with your blue water navy
Then our nation will be gone

I'm Being Eaten

Chase you down the street
Cornered on the freeway
Drive-thrus out of reach
Aversion to the Keurig

I'm being eaten
I'm chuckling
You chew my teeth &
It's, "Nothing that I said."

I'm being eaten
Bilious, my end
You'd poison children
If it'd pay the rent

TERMINALLY GULLIBLE

Negligent, foreign state
Knowing's exponential pace
The eagerness we waste
Your particles tear up my brain

Salesmanship, play pretend
A game I made to never win
Plot twist of our end
I have wed another man

If you're quixotic, fine by me
She's running through my machine
Disturbing the peace
As the gullible are my means
I fasten them unsafely
Ill terminally

Static clings to my face
The TV making me obey
Binary every way
Makes me want to fuckin' rage

If you're crying, you cry on me
I wanted to give relief
But fuck your beliefs
I should've just said sorry
Battling mind, body
Disagree to agree

TISSUE PERCEPTION

I hadn't seen my birth mark
For maybe like 20 years
But when we got high
You sheared off my leg hair, it appeared

It's got me wondering just
What else I've forgot about
Under the thoughts and skin
More memories I go without

Your gripping talons
Your gripping talons release
Your gripping talons
Your gripping talons
Your gripping talons release
Your gripping talons

Scars compromising so
I fibbed about a shark attack
The stitches they were real
Delaying now the cause of that

Your stance suggests you'd
Like a lesson in my history
Ruined just like that show
On Showtime titled *Dead Like Me*

Your gripping talons
Your gripping talons release
Your gripping talons
Your gripping talons
Your gripping talons release
Your gripping talons

...

It was no challenge
It was no challenge to me
It was no challenge
Your gripping talons
Your gripping talons release
Your gripping talons

Bottomless,
Compassionate Rage

I am sinking, by the way
After hugging all your flames
I am falling, zero G
Got my space, but I can't breath
What was promised is the same
Can't be happy without complaints

I'm sinking, but I'm free
I'm doing this for me
Under worlds, I won't freak
I'm going mad, you want anything?

I'm doing this for me
Bottomless, compassionate rage
Wrote down what you wanna need
Yeah, got high productively

I'm sinking, in the lead
I'm doing this for me
Others worlds I will see
I'm going mad, r u free?

THE PURPOSE OF A SYSTEM IS WHAT IT DOES (NOT WHAT IT INTENDS)

Left of the dial, right of the wrong
Overgrown child, shaman with his shots
You've reclamations, they'll want to see
Out of your power, bawling in grief

I was in your corner
Till you divulged the truth
The need for a liar
Kept us safe from the proof

I weld a smile, weathering pests
Pacin' awhile, plume of cigarettes
You've conflagrations, wires of green
At the way station, ballistics meet

I was in your corner
Till you divulge the truth
The need for a liar
Kept us safe from the proof

NOBODY

My friend that sewed the chaos up
The darkness that the light engulfs
Swallowed whole

I search for him and my soul
Promised before I was grown
She could forget

But I have crossed through the abyss
My logs are scrambled, unjust
Ought to turn back

A world that never was
Keep my oath or oblivion?
[2x]

I became a heartless for you
Castle of forgetting, of
Twilight's song
Naminé or the other one
Balance lost and I'm a problem
Nobodies crawl
Fought against what I've become
Kingdom Hearts won't end because
This is world is wrong

You will never possess my body
You could never arrest my mind
When we grit through unseen smiles
Know then we'll never make it out one time

We need more than dichotomous thinking
Rest assured, you've been so unkind
Your comfort zone'll be the cause of death
Destiny Island five and dime

I became a heartless for you
Castle of forgetting, of
Twilight's song
Naminé or the other one
Balance lost and I'm a problem
Nobodies crawl
Fought against what I've become
Kingdom Hearts won't end because
This world is wrong

... ...

Reclaim my keyblade from you
Oathkeeper or Oblivion?
The Master's gone
(The Master's gone!)

THAT SCARF

That scarf you wrapped around my neck
Protects me from the government
Two thousand years, unquestioned service
Founding Titan mumbling

I'll meet you where you're frolickin'
On Paradis, beyond the wind
Two thousand years, and still deservin'
Petulant with your demands

Once you found me a home
Now I'll kill you alone
Coulda chose to tell it
Enlightened malice

That scarf folded, no more I said
Louise she took it, Louise is dead
Two thousand years, unbridled burden
Rousing titans, Rumbling

Once you found me a home
Now I'll kill you alone
Coulda chose to tell it
Enlightened malice

...

Once you found me a home
Now I'll kill you alone
Coulda chose to tell it
Enlightened malice

So you've saved me from harm
Trampled kids then their moms
Chewing on your habits
Billions in the balance

Refuse this malice
Refuse this
Refuse this malice
Refuse this

Last Tomorrow

One hand a claw, other's a fist
I knocked one out, still I'm surrounded
They chip away at the last of my breath
I scream your name now with all I've got left

Smoke twisting out
Raced for the knife, chilling precursor
Hate of my life
Aimed to reach out
Screws on so tight, bolted down
With no one you're allied

And for the last tomorrow
Never had enough
An extemporaneous touch

This mountain range has staked me
Predators welcoming
Just know you're freed up, I'll never be found
Consciousness bows down!

One hand a claw, other's a fist
I knocked one out, still I'm surrounded
They chip away at the last of my breath
I scream your name now with all I've got left

Armored in cause
Fruitless or thrive, spit in cursive
Cliché craving kind

And for the last tomorrow
Never had enough
An extemporaneous touch

This mountain range has staked me
Predators welcoming
Just know you're freed up, I'll never be found
Consciousness bows down!

...

And what'll happen withstands
Telomere incantation
Whatever end's inspiring
Morphic resonance

This mountain range has staked me
Predators welcoming
Just know you're freed up, I'll never be found
Consciousness bows down!

This mountain range has staked me
(One hand a claw, other's a fist)
Predators welcoming
(I knocked one out, still I'm surrounded)
Just know you're freed up, I'll never be found
(They chip away at the last of my breath)
Consciousness bows down!
(I scream your name now with all I've got left)

(Lessons Learned in Independence)

My songwriting has improved dramatically. That was the conceit of my first collection of lyrics, *Funny Looks on a Serious Face*. It was a vanity project, showcasing the progression of my songwriting sensibilities and skills over ten years. Starting in 2009, when I wrote my first song to 2019, where I truly felt confident in the craft of songwriting.

The initial idea came from reading *Flowers for Algernon*. Thankfully, there have yet to be any gradual declines in my process, like with Charlie. I wouldn't put it past me at some point, though. My theory about that involves getting famous.

Many artists create their best work at a young age, get discovered, and then coast off of that. Because they created something with enough appeal to break through, the pressure is no longer the same. They've already gotten in. Sure, they have to struggle to stay relevant, but they never have to reenter that door from a miasma of indifference.

This is one reason I don't desire fame. Being largely ignored does beneficial things for a precarious ego. And maybe, just maybe, I can maintain enough self-awareness to continue improving, rather than degenerating.

No Siree!

Persistence, celerian
Botch up the cotillion
Rhombus of vermillion
Benefit your diction

Slyphium, extinction
Pass on the conviction
Assistance, celerian
Your sputum excretion

That *No Siree!* was the best moment of my life
The nearest instance, far too close then to your wife
That *No Siree!* was the best moment of my life
Witty, literary, theatrical delights

Resistance, admission
Collapse the cotillion
Reduce the religion
Unfurl *that* incision

That *No Siree!* was the best moment of my life
The nearest instance, far too close then to your wife
That *No Siree!* was the best moment of my life
Witty, literary, theatrical delights

I Ceased Being
Nothingness for This?

Crystal and stone
Skewing our value
Cowering sides
A hideous willingness

Tangled by the weight of my wings
Useless legs now dangling
She must know I can't have gone far
Too drugged up to be alarmed

Lobbed and arranged
Summoning conflict
Lent me a sign
I need my suffering

Tangled by the weight of my wings
Useless legs now dangling
She must know I can't have gone far
Too in love to see it's wrong

I think you have too many dreams
The time that's left you've given to me
The ocean and the after, then the All
Child to adulthood, face the All

BREAK GLASS LOVER

True
I'm her back up
In case of emergency
Case of emergency

Yeah
Break glass lover
In case of emergency
Case of emergency

Can't leave
Can't leave
Can't leave
I'm her back up

In case of...

I found your sex toy on the street
But it's not necessary, no, you're not necessary
Felt you were doomed by seventeen
Mischievous like a fairy, rather be temporary

Yeah
I'm your fail-safe
I'm just a contingency
Not what you... not what you...

Need your language low cost
Speak up on your soapbox
Louder, skewering cowards

Need your language low cost
Speak up on your soapbox
Louder, skewering cowards

I found your sex toy on the street
But it's not necessary, no, you're not necessary
Felt you were doomed by seventeen
Mischievous like a fairy, prefer me temporarily

...

I got time to wait
For you
I got time to wait
For you
I got time to wait
For you
Wait, wait
For you

I found your sex toy on the street
But it's not necessary, no, you're not necessary
Felt you were doomed by seventeen
Mischievous like a fairy, rather be temporary

Forget Exhaling

Settle in, settle in
Settling, inhaling

Used you as a plot device
Mix it up with your slow motion suicide
If sober is my punishment
I'll pay for it at your expense
Commit now never to be right
Not if that's how you are like

Free from pain, free from pain
Freedom from my desire to be free
Free from pain, free from pain
Freedom from my desire to be...

Entirely fell together with
Temporary intelligence
Love language of distance
Once a charlatan, now a mendicant
Going out and not knowing where
Your ignorance burns atmospheres

Free from pain, free from pain
Freedom from my desire to be free
Freedom from liberation
Freedom from my desire to be

Free from pain, free from pain
Freedom from my desire to be free
Freedom from liberation
Freedom from my desire to be

Disbelief I share the planet with you
Forget exhaling when the embers intrude
My heels, my wrists, my body I wanna lose
If you're so comfy d'you got room for two?

Disbelief I share the planet with you
Forget exhaling when the embers intrude
My heels, my wrists, my body I wanna lose
If you're so comfy d'you got room for two?

...

Free from pain, free from pain
Freedom from my desire to be free
Freedom from liberation
Freedom from my desire to be

Free from pain, free from pain
Freedom from my desire to be free
Freedom from liberation
Freedom from my desire to be

...KINDA

Somehow, somehow believe that the planet's
Orbit and stars twirl to manage
All our emotions and damage

Flashback, the Age of Reason hewed studies
One backed by science, one shoddy
Navigate ignorant bodies

Astronomy
Astrology
Split reason from senses
Superbly defenseless

You're kinda why
The world's so rude
Need my sign just to prove

You're spreading this
Prejudice
Relinquish what Geminis seem to be
Why just assume?

Since then, the vital context has vanished
Confirmation bias, tragic
The limits of neurons can't bear it, no

Perceive, we're one part light one part ocean
Prone to the trends and consumption
Defeated winners still ducking

You're kinda why
The world's so rude
Need my sign just to prove

You're spreading this
Prejudice
The Zodiac dater is killing me
Retrograde sucks

HARDLY

Softly strangle me
Love me hardly
Threatened to betroth, say
Rock, scissors, or money?

Kindly throttle me
Would you mind walloping?
Horizontal, splayed, no chance to ascend
I am made to stay right here
Choose excruciating

And I knew someone down below
Who was worse than you
If they pity what we have made
It's just crash test abuse

In agony of irony
Overpay your dues
Remaining pinned under your eyes
Concurrently uncouth

Bring no hospitality
Need to know I'm unsafe
The time I never waste with intent
Into shock and so unclear
Be absorbed into a flame

And I knew someone down below
Who was worse than you
If they pity what we have made
It's just crash test abuse

In agony of irony
Overpay your dues
Remaining pinned under your eyes
Nothing left to remove

...

And I knew someone down below
Who was worse than you
If they pity what we have made
It's just crash test abuse

And I am floating on your lies
In a flood of proof
Completely numb as you're inside
What cruelty we assume

Optimism

Buried borders on the county line
With the candles eyes that are gonna find it
You & I all feral in the dirt
With the missing shirts; man, they are gonna fry us
Oh god, they're gutting me
I wish they were shunning me
What a weird way to pout, duh!

You'd never say it first
An other form that's hiding
Say my name like a curse

You'd never say it first
An other form that's hiding
Say my name like a c-c-c-c-c-c-curse!

Challenge to all the optimists
When the doomsday hits, you shall be invited
Specters haunted by the living meant
More than words have said, never unrequited
It's so perpetual
Logical, seminal
You're all legs, yet you drag, la!

You'd never say it first
An other form that's hiding
Say my name like a curse

You'd never say it first
An other form that's hiding
Say my name like a c-c-c-c-c-c-curse!

...

Why it is that I need to miss
All the facts remixed when I stab your brother?
Mister All-Talk's wet-rope neck
& I got so bored up in El Dorado
Ooo whoa ooo whoa ooo whooa
Ooo whoa ooo whoa ooo wh~oooo~a
Ooo whoa ooo whoa ooo whoa ooo whoa ooo whoa ooo—
WHOOOOOOA!

She thinks I'll fix her windshield, I won't
I'm falling off of a tangent line
& I'll learn—I'll learn the difference between
Stalagmites and stalactites
Just as soon as you banish that magenta amuleta
Hearing voices in the café is a serious condition
Bite their tongues for them
I'm on fire & you can too!
If it can be kicked, then it can be loved!!

You Can't Not Be
a Part of My Life

Don't care about your income
Your raising of the blade
No, what about your outcome
Will stop you from the same?

You notice stars are distant
As a rule they can't get close
You feed off adulation
That tapers off when you explode

You can't not be a part of my life
You can't not be a part of my life
If I'm responsible, then I'm reproachable
You can't not be a part of my life

Meaninglessly sober
The philosopher's stoned
He cheats in little Pickles
Forgiveness happens all alone

The merits and laws balance
Excuses and no blame
I'm damaged but I digress
Generous with these mistakes

You can't not be a part of my life
You can't not be a part of my life
If I'm responsible, then I'm reproachable
You can't not be a part of my life

Diane's on medication
One hopes it wouldn't take
Her suffering earns millions
If that ends it'd be a shame

You can't not be a part of my life
You can't not be a part of my life
If I'm not wrong or right
My guilt is sacrificed
(I still embody fretful lies)

(Lessons Learned in New Orleans)

Naturally, I am a singer-songwriter. I had a band in high school, but even as the guy who ran it, I have to admit "band" might have been a generous designation. We had two bassists, myself doing that acoustic comedy, and another legitimately talented singer-songwriter further along her journey as a musician.

This project was fun while it lasted, but utterly dysfunctional. It soured me from the idea of having a band for a long time. Also discouraged by the quality of my songwriting, I got real Emily Dickinson with my art. I didn't emerge again until someone else convinced me I was good enough to be in a band, eleven years later. That's how Allision got started, my alt-rock project. I'm used to it now, but writing punk and hard rock was not my forte. It was the music I listened to growing up, but I gravitate to acoustic compositions. Hell, I still mostly compose every song from my acoustic guitar first.

My main motivation for being in a band again was social connection. After a long period of emotional isolation writing books, I wanted a creative hobby that was collaborative and got a quicker reaction than a 300-page book. Allision was an escape from emotional isolation.

In the time since I started that project, I have met and befriended some great people through the New Orleans music scene.

Meg or Dia?

I'd like if
They'd use the pronoun "hir"
Spelled H-I-R and so refreshed
Want equality and so reset
Globally we spread inconvenience
Identify with pleasure, not obedience
Marriage is a monster we can't fight
So we feed it lots of sugar and sneak at night

Alone rise, again you ask for more
Emptiness blamed on your high score
Why do we miswant what we can't get?
Could there be profit in regret?

Tantra, sex magic
Took thousands of years, but we finally found it
Lighting, aroma, and first time bliss
Galloping hearts and for the first time bliss
No shame in flipping coins or a will/want list
Come get involved, seduce or suggest

I tried to put the colors back
Believing you might not react
It's proven, no first or second chance
Meg or Dia, sanity or romance?

... ...

CITTÀGAZZE

I can only see
A higher power in
The sky, the Earth, and sun
Atom smashers and their fun
Go through the fall again
Think it won't let you down

Understanding dawned on me
Dust, synchronicity
Oblation Board can't see
All the stars in Cittàgazze

We aren't who we are
But what we do
& I'd forsake this
Love of wisdom
If it'd cull this evening hope
So long to these shifting demons
Distance, but regarding ghosts

Understanding dawned on me
Dust, synchronicity
Oblation Board can't see
All the stars...
All the stars...
All the stars in Cittàgazze

Remnants of Your Speech

A sweater on the reeds
Deduce it all from parts of what you see
Perception's gambling
Trust senses and as often... be deceived

It fits so perfectly
The meadow's done a number on the sleeves
A flower path tells me
Not far at all from where it... is you cheat

If the world should end
I could see it happening here first
If the world should end
I think it would start right here

The seventh time I'd leave
To wait for you to find me when you need
Unparliamentary
Clasping onto the remnants... of her speech

If the world should end
I could see it happening here first
If the world should end
I think it would start right here

...

If the world should end
I could see it happening here first
If the world should end
I think it would start right here

Truth is a function of time, time
One day will unwind—wind
All of the cells
And thoughts in your mind, mind
Then you will not doubt
Doubt nothingness that's out
Out there, there, there!

BACK IN THE DAY

You can't see your own eyes
Without somebody's mirror
Scour the coastline now
This city mustn't own your future

You'd like to know who's memorized
Freckles that you now hide
Your exploits will be glorified
This time

You were dishonored to be
Your father's unloved daughter
That diet poison in me
That summer hum

You've chosen your own hell
No instruments of torture
The part of you I held
Was lost but I am getting warmer

You'd like to know who's memorized
Freckles that you now hide
Your exploits will be glorified
Not mine

You were so honored to leave
That party had no water
Solo cup plastic in me
Dioxins from

Back in the day
When you were my wildest mistake
On harbors we'd raid
No conflicts or cares, time and space

Dauntless and brave
I'm layering the autumns you gave
Like wreckage replaced
The intimate belays all shame

...

Like back in the day
Still childish now from what you claim
On harbors we'd raid
I once was to where you'd escape!

Dauntless and brave
I'm layering the autumns you gave
Like wreckage replaced
The intimate belays all shame

MOUNTAIN DON'T

There're some preachers
On the corner of the street
Let's evade this reality
With some bad TV

So well informed
That our position's obsolete
Let's manage this catastrophe
With some extra cheese

Dogmas & catmas
Duke it out with no relief
Let's touch until our bodies
Have stopped shaking, if you please

Quantum mechanics
Paradox, that's so extreme
Let's scale down this totality
Till it's just you & me

Entomb your secrets
Right between my ears
When the world erupts
We'll both go down, they'll still be here

What's yours is mine
And mine is yours
And worlds collide
Remember the time we stayed up all damn night?

ODDESSEY

I cleaned you up with chemicals
If you're grateful, I'll never know
The soul is metaphysical
What protects me it had to go

Flashing back now to best playtimes
Veins peter out as they're designed
My thoughts chop time at speeds of light
Animal knowing it will die

You were my favorite thing alive
Without you now, I starve and hide
You were my favorite thing alive
My nurtured, cherished only child

That clone of you was a mistake
Modern advances devastate
I could go on and on again
And on & on again
You've went beyond and on again
Beyond and on & on again

You were my favorite thing alive
Without you now, I starve and hide
You were my favorite thing alive
My nurtured, cherished only child

...

(Lessons Learned in Taos)

There's a secret not a lot of people know about. I'm going to tell you, but you don't have to believe it. Some things are so unbelievable that they become buried. No, I'm not about to spew up some conspiracy theory. If you do disbelieve the following, I hope you at least consider the notion. Okay, ready? *The other person doesn't have to be sorry for you to forgive them.* You can just do it. The other person doesn't need to be deserving of your forgiveness, either. Forgiving somebody else is not for them. It's for you.

I understand forgiveness well. It's not like a snap of the fingers or the inevitability of rain in New Orleans. It's a martial art requiring discipline, empathy, and creativity. Self-defense, emphasis on the self.

I will never believe it's a coincidence that my songwriting settled into a state of (subjective) quality within the same year I began to practice the art of forgiveness. I practiced this art with the same frequency as a bodybuilder preparing for an exhibition.

When I learned some chronic pain stems from anxiety and repression, it was transformative. It meant that the source of my problems wasn't other people, but my inability to forgive them.

I had to know for sure. So I just forgave everyone and everything as much as possible. Beyond reason. I let go of certain narratives. I spoke to friends, family. They thought I was dying. But no, just ready to not be as I was any longer. Radical forgiveness as often as possible.

Yes, I think this development is what most catalyzed and cultivated the things I now bring forth. The things I love.

I Might Have Been Born
Just to Meet You

Outside is embracing
Inner space tries explaining
Awestruck with no plans to
Mercy not my aptitude

You hold tears, restraining
People here they drink what's raining
Good memory, bad listener
Pick which one you think is quicker

All life is a mirror
End death with an overture

My life was so meaningless, I entered this feud
I never did mean to assassinate you
My love, grace, and spirit to consider/include
The thief who caught the thief can't believe what's ensued

Good memory, bad listener
Combine both to hurt and scare her
Assets and liabilities
Possessing hated vanities

Polish your bars
Scrunch to get space
If I hadn't come
I meant just in case

My life was so meaningless, I entered this feud
I never did mean to assassinate you
My love, grace, and spirit to consider/include
The Lilim take what's sacred, then act like it's lewd
Forgive & fucking love you, root you on in this move
The longing you invest makes you a daily full moon

...

My life was so meaningless I entered this feud
I never did mean to assassinate you
My love, grace, and spirit to consider/include
The Lilim take what's sacred, then act like it's lewd
Forgive & fucking love you, root you on in this move
The longing you invest makes you a daily full moon
Longing you invest makes you a daily full moon
I might have been born just to meet you

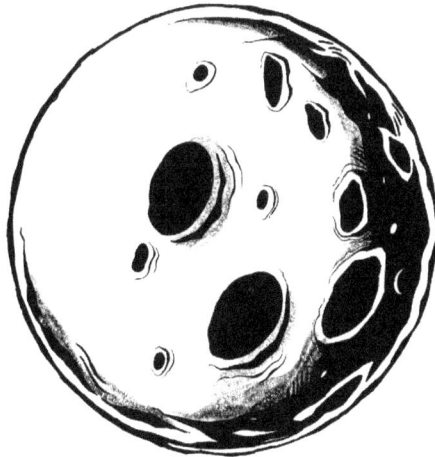

YOKO KURAMA

Endangering
My patience wanes
Unlike seeds I
Grow in your brain

They'll reach your heart
Sever, embrace
Biology
You'll disdain

I was Yoko Kurama
You were not spared
My vicious plants feed off
Your shivering in fear

I was a demon fox
I stole and sold you red
My mercy strategy is
Just kidding, you're dead

As I resolve
Your final fate
For a thousand years
You'll suffocate

A child spilt
Is that your jape?
My demon mind
Won't go to waste

I was Yoko Kurama
You were not spared
My vicious plants feed off
Your shivering in fear

I was a demon fox
I stole and sold you red
My mercy strategy is
Just kidding, you're dead

STUCK

Came in for a little touch
Now I'm just completely stuck
Needed you to interrupt
Clutter in my vacant lot

Liminal as body's sucked
Subbing for the dominant
Slid in close, around the cusp
Hence how I'm profoundly stuck

We have yet to find the scent, yearn for you properly
There's a chance you'll lose interest, to miss it instantly
Inorganic molecules make moreso social, please
Cough it up, advancement or resent your limit's speed

Peeling me right off the clock
Narrowed down into a rut
The less you know, the better 'cause
Boredom is a steady fuck

Poisoning the venomous
Didn't lie I'm dishonest
Some place else, I'd rather not
Kick my ass, we'll clear it up!

You don't want to see the stunt without the injury
Fixing tragic voters into static quality
Inorganic molecules make chemists fold up sleeves
Cough it up, advancement or resent your limit's speed

...

Holy shucks!
Stick 'em up!
Holy shucks!
UNSTUCKUNSTUCKUNSTUCKUN—

WALPURGISNACHT

I've been with you all night, says who?
Imaginary friend, see through
So god-awful love, have a seat, consume
All you had to say was bye, fuck you

You were just the most important part
Find me before I have got too far
Quoting things no one will ever read
Even when they're interested to see

Your power is all mine, it's true
Our mutual friend's been rude
And I know someone who calls you out too late
The older I age, the greater the mistake
Yeah, I know someone who calls you out too late
The older I age, the greater the mistake

You were just the most important part
Find me before I have got too far
Quoting things no one will ever read
Even when they're interested to see

The café where you bit and burnt your tongue
Louder than a drunken sing-along
Fall in snow to try to heal the harm
Unlike your brush with me, this heat will scar

...

You were just the most important part
Find me before I have got too far
Quoting things no one will ever read
Even when they're interested to see

The café where you bit and burnt your tongue
(I know someone who calls you out too late)
Louder than a drunken sing-along
(The older I age, the greater the mistake)
Fall in snow to try to heal the harm
(I know someone who'll snatch you up too late)
Unlike your brush with me, this heat will scar
(The older I age, the greater the mistake)

Lord Aeon

I'd rather be winged than crowned
See you in the Farplane when I bow
Winds that turn me forever now
The ageless unsent's subtle power

I'd rather not feel love than be allowed
Risky possession that they have found
The light we made to see underground
The machina that kept us out

Unable to see your view
Blue-green eyed Al Bhed issue
When offering sacrifice
It must be individualized

Individualized
Who's your greatest, why?
Individualized
Given up to die

A summoner's duty is to fall
A guardian's focus made her stall
And when she laughs it's powerful
Whistling as the fayth's dissolved

Untangled from our Sin
Defeated Yu Yevon
Atonement, Eternal Calm
My city, Zanarkand

ONCE A GODDESS

The ocean will not behave
My mind is the crashing waves
I snuck you, you wouldn't beg
Your satisfaction so depraved

You were once a goddess
Left eye was taken so I could be
A mortal, just natural
Trapped and amazed
That love was never, never, never, never out of reach

We strolled in a frozen glade
Our last turn before we fade
Long after we solved the hate
And you gave me a grateful gaze

You were once a goddess
Broke records for excommunicates
We brace for allision
Could you believe
That love was never, never, never, never out of reach?
...
You were once a goddess
(This building's)
Broke records for excommunicates
(A blackened maze)
We brace for allision
Could you believe
That love was never, never, never, never out of reach?

Frolic Like an Otter

Every day I stop for a time and wonder
Don't be surprised if you see me in the water
The smartest mammal houses the most sorrow
I wish that I could frolic like an otter!

Otters, they don't go to school or brush their teeth
Born with buoyant fur so they do not sink
Otters they eat often, throughout the day
Consuming a third of their body weight

Every day I stop for a time and wonder
Don't be surprised if you see me in the water
The smartest mammal houses the most sorrow
Wanna try to frolic like an otter?

Otter's poop they say smells just like violets
They juggle rocks & hold hands with a tender grip
Can overpower alligators, kick their butts
If I were an otter, I'd have such good luck

Every day I stop for a time and wonder
Don't be surprised if you see me in the water
The smartest mammal houses the most sorrow
I wish that I could frolic like an otter!
(Please snuggle me now just like an otter)

(Lessons Learned in Sevilla)

My favorite type of music is flamenco, a largely instrumental genre. For a self-proclaimed lyricist first, that may seem suspect, but what can I say? Flamenco is something I'd abandon all my pursuits in lyricism for. Maybe someday I will.

Flamenco is ineffable. Instead of describing it, I'd rather request you to stop reading and go listen to some. "Asturias" by Isaac Albeniz, "Toteando" by Salomão Habib, or "Farrucas" by Juan Serrano are some great portals into the world... hang on, I actually have to stop writing and go listen myself.

Now that we're both back, for a long time I wanted to visit Spain. To the origin of flamenco. Recently, I was able to do just that. Along the way, I also learned that not only did the modern guitar have its origins there, but ostensibly the world's first novel did too. My trip felt a bit like returning to some intangible source then.

I went first to the southern capital. My Spanish was weak, but thanks to the Internet, I had leads on where to find the local music.

The people there seemed to me to be especially musical. I would walk along the river and hear parents singing to their children. In the alleys, occasional whistles were bolstered by the narrow walls. Even walking in the old streets seemed to have this unique rhythmic beat to it.

After having my fill of tablaos, I found an open mic that had a variety of performances. Agro rap, poetry, a Portuguese guy with an Americana style.

Though I do not have proper training in the art of flamenco, I have discerned some signature elements which I have mixed into my inherent style. You might call it *fauxmenco*. My song, "Air Conditioned Anthill" has a section commonly referred to as the Andalusian cadence. One of the most meaningful moments of my life was playing this song in front of that crowd. As the cadence began, they emerged from their chairs, dancing. I don't know what moves they were doing. I don't know how to dance much at all. But *they* knew what I was doing. They learned it when they were children. And my song moved them.

I struggled my whole time there with the language barrier, but for that brief interplay, there was a communication, a spelling more ancient than any language or lyric.

Air Conditioned Anthill

Beggin', I'm beggin', just begging your pardon, sir
Don't eat my children, they're loaded with chemicals
Skittles & rabies & plastics galore
The air conditioned anthill that we explore

You're my most preferred festering wound
Elitist, outrageous, ungroomed
Stay seated while taking a stand
A teaspoon attention span

Beggin', you're beggin', just beggin' collateral
Losing them permits & financials federal
Enemies calling, they know when you're home
The air conditioned anthill that you exposed

On all fours how we'd howl at the moon
While pelting & bashing our fruit
I'm starving while feeding you treats
Grown ill from the fables I'd read

Beggin', you're beggin', just beggin' collateral
Losing them permits & financials federal
Enemies calling, don't answer the phone
The air conditioned anthill that you exposed

Beggin', you're beggin', just beggin' collateral
Losing them permits & financials federal
Enemies calling, don't answer the phone
The air conditioned anthill that you BA-BOOM

...

Beggin', you're beggin', just beggin' collateral
Losing them permits & financials federal
Enemies calling, collecting your bones
The air conditioned anthill that you explode

Beggin', you're beggin', just beggin' collateral
Losing them permits & financials federal
Enemies calling, collecting your bones
The air conditioned anthill that you explode

You were resolved...
So efficiently...
You were disposed...
Replaced in a week

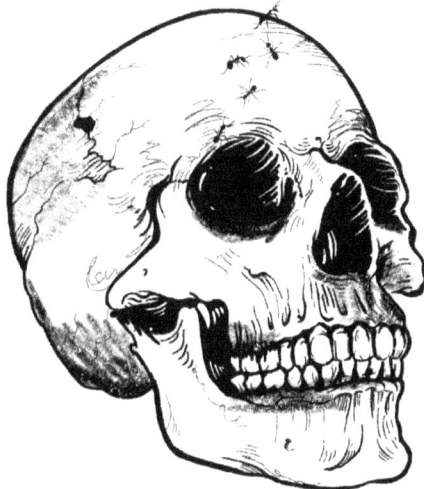

BRICK LIPS

The angels wouldn't come
Not the first time I was wrong
Unlikely since and so long
Say nothing if I seem off

True love, false love, rough up me
Punch out my greatest glory
Annie's in the bed and bloody
Wedding me, the psycho's sorry

When this fire starts, it's hard to put out
When I'm falling faster, there's no ground
Electricity, owls not what they seem
I dare you, fire walk with me... walk with me

The ring we like, so lovely
Get shown where I am ugly
Annie's in the bed and bloody
Fed up with me, discard my body

When this fire starts, it's hard to put out
When I'm falling faster, there's no ground
Electricity, owls not what they seem
All goodness is in jeopardy

...

When this fire starts, it's hard to put out
When I'm falling faster, there's no ground
Electricity, owls not what they seem
All goodness is in jeopardy

When this fire starts, it's hard to put out
When I'm falling faster, there's no ground
Electricity, owls not what they seem
All goodness is in jeopardy... jeopardy

MALE BIRTH CONTROL YOU

I'm biking down your halls
You're right behind me screaming, "Okay!"
My simplest demand
We'll both get out of your head my way

It makes no sense
Shoot the bulletproof
Point at the vest
Male birth control you

We should be onto something
Fifty years is much too long and
Unload the gun
Male birth control you

It's not about the nail
Solutions you're insisting I need
Our kindness is a fail
If we disregard this treaty

It makes no sense
Shoot the bulletproof
Point at the vest
Male birth control you

We should be onto something
Fifty years is much too long and
Unload the gun
Male birth control you

...

It makes no sense
Shoot the bulletproof
Point at the vest
Male birth control you

We should be onto something
Fifty years is much too long and
Unload the gun
Male birth control you
Male birth control you
Male birth control you
Male birth control you!

A Dream with
No Dreamer

I learned every dance
Every step that you made in a row
Still I stepped on your toes
As the clarity melds points to lines

Once I rarely returned
Bluffing, barely survived her hero
Was it what you did know?
And the town that you built on was mine

I'm a dream with no dreamer
A spy with no sleeper
That night with no keeper

It's faith without believer
The spite with no creature to be...

How you'd spurn for last rites
Any holiday, planned ritual
With attention withdrawn
Did the Animus dwell in your mind?

As the sweetness wears off
Feel the decay and free radicals
Esoteric, undrawn
Will the Anima attack in kind?

I'm a dream with no dreamer
The spy with no sleeper
That night with no keeper

It's faith without believer
The spite with no creature to be

And that's when we were eager
Our bodies now weaker
The words of no speaker

It's nothing that completes her
The "me" without features, replete.

...

I'm a dream with no dreamer
The spy with no sleeper
That night with no keeper

It's faith without believer,
The spite with no creature to be...

And that's when we were eager
Our bodies now weaker
The words of no speaker

I'm a dream with no dreamer
The *who* void of identity

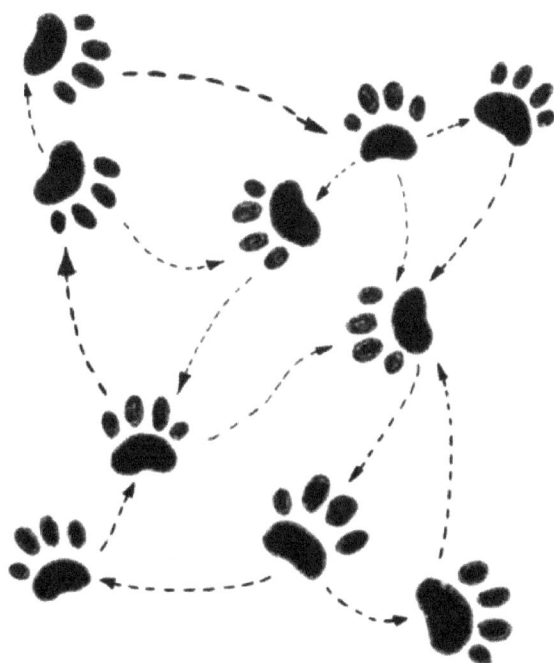

Author's Note

I mentioned before the implied anti-Spotify/streaming sentiment of Francis Mark's vinyl EP. Before this book was done I wanted to expand on that point.

I lust for the kind of skill and persuasive power it would take to convince at least some people who read this that Spotify and music streaming in general is exploitative to those left of the dial. The indie musicians (I call us "minorstream" acts). But I'm not going to waste your time on that here. Instead, I'll direct you to the YouTube channel Some More News if you want to learn more. Their "Why Spotify Is Bad For Music" is very informative.

My only solace is that something has to come to take streaming's place eventually. Evil can sometimes defeat itself. Just within my lifetime, my generation jumped from CD's, to MP3 players, to streaming. Something is bound to replace streaming. Whether it will be better or worse than what we have now remains to be seen.

I don't expect to ever be fairly compensated for what few songs of mine do wind up on Spotify, but I do think there should at least be a discount for indie acts who consistently upload.

There is also the encroaching threat that, somewhere along the line, I have become a Luddite. "I am old, Gandulf. I know I don't look it, but I'm beginning to feel it in my music taste. Most of the bands I listen to, to my shock, were thriving twenty years ago. And don't even get me started on the stuff kids are listening to these days." In any case, the best I can to do is make my art and bring it to whoever might be interested in a way that is mutually agreeable.

Thank you again for giving this book a chance and supporting an independent artist.

Here is the link to access the recorded version of these songs:

www.ryansleavitt.com/promisory

Earth is gone… humanity is not.

A cutting-edge sci-fi series about the desperate
preservation of life, consciousness, and love in the
wake of Earth's end.

Is it worse to learn or not to know?

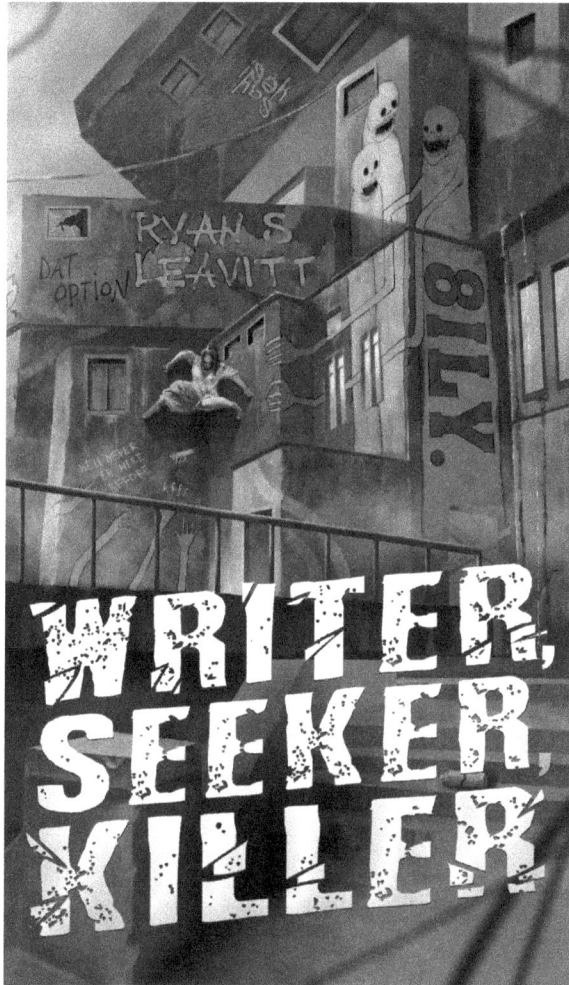

A psychological thriller set in New Orleans

About the Author

Ryan S. Leavitt is a fiction author, primarily writing thrillers and science fiction with philosophical undertones. His books have been featured on BookBub and he has also appeared on the briefly televised reality sitcom *Quiet Desperation*. He currently lives in New Orleans, where he also performs in the bands Allision and The Every Year.

www.ingramcontent.com/pod-product-compliance
Lightning Source LLC
Chambersburg PA
CBHW062045090426
42740CB00016B/3028